Dash and Crash!

By Carmel Reilly

T0360180

The school bell rang
for lunch.

"I will dash out to play
with Frank!" said Tash.

Tash ran down the steps.

But she did not see
the trash bin.

Crash! Smash!

Tash fell and got a gash
on her hand.

Mr Brash ran to Tash.

"I can fix that gash
in a flash, Tash," he said.

Tash sat and put out her hand.

Mr Brash fixed the gash.

Tash met Frank.

"Mr Brash fixed my gash!" Tash said.

They had fun, and then the bell rang.

"Let's dash back to school!"
said Tash.

"Tash! Do **not** dash!"
said Frank.

CHECKING FOR MEANING

1. What did Tash crash into? *(Literal)*

2. Who helped Tash? *(Literal)*

3. Why do you think Tash likes to dash? *(Inferential)*

EXTENDING VOCABULARY

gash	What does the word *gash* mean? What is another word with a similar meaning? Why do you think the author chose to use the word *gash* instead of another word?
Mr	Look at the word *Mr.* What does it mean? What is it short for? What other words can be used to formally address people?
It's	Look at the word *It's.* What two words is *It's* short for? Find another contraction in the text. What two words were put together to make *Let's?*

MOVING BEYOND THE TEXT

1. What might you need to do to treat a gash?

2. In what situations might someone dash from one place to another?

3. What can you do to make sure that you move safely around your school?

4. What do you think the message of this story is?

SPEED SOUNDS

at	an	ap	et	og	ug

ell	ack	ash	ing

PRACTICE WORDS

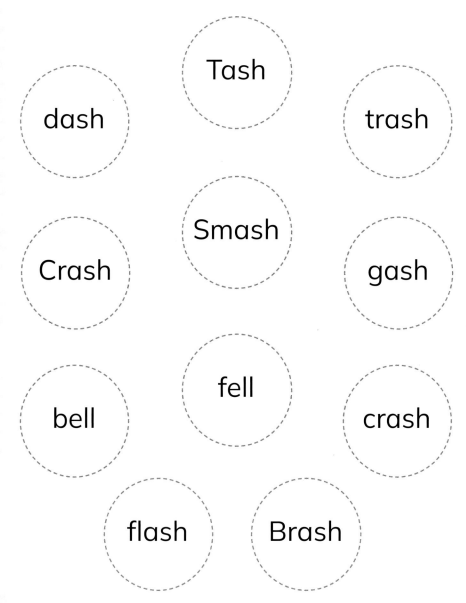

Tash

dash

trash

Smash

Crash

gash

fell

bell

crash

flash

Brash